RISING, FALLING, HOVERING

ALSO BY C.D. WRIGHT

C.D. WRIGHT

Rising, Falling, Hovering

 Copper Canyon Press

Port Townsend, Washington

Grateful acknowledgment is made to the editors of the following publications, in which some of these poems first appeared: *The Believer, Conjunctions, Kilometer Zero, The New Yorker, NO,* Octopus, and *Verse.* Special thanks to the *Chicago Review* for printing in its entirety the title poem, "Rising, Falling, Hovering," across two issues.

Some of the poems included here were previously collected in *Like Something Flying Backwards: New and Selected Poems* (Bloodaxe Books Ltd., 2007).

Cover art: Monoprint by Denny Moers

Copper Canyon Press is in residence at Fort Worden State Park in Port Townsend, Washington, under the auspices of Centrum. Centrum is a gathering place for artists and creative thinkers from around the world, students of all ages and backgrounds, and audiences seeking extraordinary cultural enrichment.

LIBRARY OF CONGRESS CATALOGING-IN-PUBLICATION DATA

Wright, C.D.
Rising, falling, hovering / C.D. Wright.
  p.   cm.
ISBN 978-1-55659-273-7 (alk. paper)
I. Title.
PS3573.R497R57 2008
811'.54—dc22

2007038304

98765432

COPPER CANYON PRESS
Post Office Box 271
Port Townsend, Washington 98368
www.coppercanyonpress.org

for Pura López-Colomé
and
for Valerie Mejer Caso

Contents

El respeto al derecho ajeno es la paz.

BENITO JUÁREZ

The momentum of existence towards others,
towards the future, towards the world can be
restored as a river unfreezes.

MAURICE MERLEAU-PONTY

RISING, FALLING, HOVERING

Re: Happiness, in pursuit thereof

It is 2005, just before landfall.
Here I am, a labyrinth, and I am a mess.
I am located at the corner of Waterway
and Bluff. I need your help. You will find me
to the left of the graveyard, where the trees
grow especially talkative at night,
where fog and alcohol rub off the edge.
We burn to make one another sing;
to stay the lake that it not boil, earth
not rock. We are running on Aztec time,
fifth and final cycle. Eyes switch on/off.
We would be mercurochrome to one another
bee balm or chamomile. We should be concrete,
glass, and spandex. We should be digital or,
at least, early. Be ivory-billed. Invisible
except to the most prepared observer.
We will be stardust. Ancient tailings
of nothing. Elapsed breath. No,
we must first be ice. Be nails. Be teeth.

Be lightning.

Like Having a Light at Your Back You Can't See but You Can Still Feel (1)

As if it were streaming into your ear.

The edges of a room long vanished.

She is not really hearing what he's really saying.

The shine is going out of the ground
but they are sure of their footing.

It's not that they have been here before, but
they are young and they have water.

There are masses of rose hips and they are noisy.

The forward direction requires almost no effort.

Consonant with this feeling of harmony
comes another, less comfortable.

Not of being lost but of not belonging.

Yet they were not covering the air
with false words.

They moved along without talking,
not touching.

They wore their own smell.

She tastes salt and they must be getting closer.

Others are out there who are drifting.

If this took place anywhere near the presidential palace

it would be nonstop terrifying.

And this could be the reason she has started to scream.

Like Hearing Your Name Called in a Language
You Don't Understand

Since the day the bell was cast

I have sat in the bishop's carved chair and waited my turn

with my feet crossed at the ankles, and the leather of my huaraches

cutting into the hide of my foot.

From where I was sitting I watched the light being drawn off

the magnolias in the Plaza de Armas

while the voices of the others choired an evening.

I have risen to the lectern when the eyes of the host summoned.

I faced the great open doors as the faces of strangers
acknowledged their own losses.

I saw the white trousers of the vendor flapping in the dust

his body engulfed in balloons,

the children selling Chiclets dispersed;

the shoeshine boy putting away his brushes, the sum of his inheritance.

I have read what was written there, said, Gracias, and sat down again.

I have climbed the pyramidal steps and felt winded and humbled.

I have stood small and borracha and been glad
of not being thrown down the barranca alongside the pariah consul
in the celebrated book.

In every sense have I felt lonelier than a clod of clay, a whip, a bolsa,
a skull of chocolate.

I have been lured by my host's pellucid face and the blue salvia
where the rooster is buried.

Though I have worn the medal of the old town with forlorn pleasure
I say unto you:

Comrades, be not in mourning for your being

to express happiness and expel scorpions is the best job on earth.

Rising, Falling, Hovering

Rising, Falling, Hovering

                               Yesterday

nothing was unusual   a rainy March morning

there were scores of starlings on the ground

she had been thinking about what he said

                       What has been said is said often

Sifting for some interlinear significance   on the pallid grass

the birds   accumulated chromatic density

He stopped her (not vice versa) in the rain to tell her

he had been thinking   the voice beginning to dematerialize

against the slur of cars

               neither of them moving just yet

In the vapor light of the park

it felt as if the trees were walking with them

as if they had passed into a cloud   she had to ask him

       if this were living or

Never having seen him in fog

which set off his eyes   his voice as spectral

as he looked   his look spectral as neon in fog

                    The door stuck

on the threshold   electricals on the blink

the curtains eliminated the houses on the hill

cold as mirrors   this rain   wood unwilling to catch

                    Locked in the time-suck of another

they talked and then fucked and then talked

and fucked and it was like that   grown-up   yet unrehearsed

He would appear central in her book   then go off

on his own   meanwhile   no one but themselves

in the kitchen's recessed lighting   in their underpants

Drinking warm beer   not taking calls

she had no idea   who was calling   kept calling

                    ringing in the emptiness

I know how you feel   he lied   I know you do

she lied   but to listen   just to listen   tantamount

to forgiveness   it did not matter for what

The longer one lived   the less to forgive

The air changed around them   her face

betrayed her face   she thought more about before

when not much was more than enough

                a pair of cutoffs on a salvaged couch

They wore the scent of smokers then

He rode in front   He said nothing   She drove

He looked out over the water as they crossed the bridge

It was all but dark   he took a pen out of his shirt pocket

and wrote something down

                        he cared not to share with her

Her bags had not been in anyone else's possession

Her bracelets set off the metal detector

On the moving sidewalk   she studied his back

through its thin cloth

Him with the scar   do not think him healed

(so the proverb warns)

A funnel of feelings   about going anywhere

during a war

Are your ears popping

trying to make light talk   his half-delineated face

already in twilight   the batting pouring

from clouds below

Were you ever told   the soul detaches from its earthly body

at around 40,000 feet

If they handed you the black box

what would you bequeath

trying to make light talk

He slept with the dead then   nothing roused him

Did she mention a missing spleen   had she warned him

she shaved down there   the night before

One glimpse of the paper was too much

the number of their dead to remain unknown

So the sleepless one hectored the sleeper:

About the other night   I know you are sorry   I am sorry too   We were tired   Me

and my open-shut-case mouth   You and your clockwork disciplines   And I know it is

too far to go   But we can't leave it to the forces to rub out the color of the world

What is said has been said before   This is no time for poetry

When the laborer picked up the statue of the santo

    he heard a fluttering and picked a petal off his arm

If the shoes of children are good luck

    what about the boots of a brown-eyed soldier

In his hut the old man loved the mystique of radio

    it took him somewhere irreligious and refrigerated

If they come here he told the much younger woman   Keep still

    make yourself small   make yourself smaller

Posing to look proud on the old burro

    though his mounts had always been thoroughbred

Asked if she had a memory of the camphor-drenched gown

    hung as netting   above the matrimonial hammock

Not really she said   I know I wore it once

    on the other side   al otro lado   and I was smaller then

I have the grey-blue eyes of my gachupín forebears

    but don't take me for one of them

Then: on a certain night and no other

another telegenic war begins.

Can you describe this.

I cannot. This is not the day or the hour.

The color is all wrong.

What dreams I had.

You too.

We were going the speed of night.

We were riding black dogs.

So? What?

So. I don't know.

A plane set down under a bowl of blueness against a ragged ridge. The old
Zapotec town aroused by the onset of evening. The shuttle bus rumbling from airstrip
to zocalo. Swallows silhouetted, then bats against sporadic streetlamps. Lilt of children.
Dogs barking at exhaust pipes. Passport of origin jostled out of mind. Unlit stairs. A worn
lobby off a keyed-up corner. Walls colored by water from a tank of angel fish, the same
                                        ghoulish glow from a muted TV.
        Civilian limbs sticking out of wreckage like so much rebar. Baghdad's thirteen-
century chronicle

                            shelled into the memory hole.

Heat radiating from burning books. Evidence of ago gone.

What has been unloosed cannot be leashed.

What has been stolen will be sold.

    From their louvered window on the mezzanine, the stark, darkened hill. From the roof, view over septic tank of the stark, darkened hill; flounce of jacaranda in the zocalo.

    Who has been torn from one son will be forlorned of another.
            These are the sandals that bore the rubbings of his skin. By this slough, they knew him.

    Who has been silenced cannot be unsilenced.

    The number of their dead to remain unknown.

    Him with the scar   Do not think him healed

¿Mande?

Nada.

¿Mande?

Nada.

                                to be cont.

One bright night: we will see through the oaths of threat and protection

We will get out of our white cars in our white dresses

We will join the black dogs in a circle of the light

We will turn in the circle of the night

Memory murdered

Not so; instead:

They are spared the television except in passing through the lobby. She struggles with the dailies in Spanish. BÁRBARO ATAQUE: MÁS DE MIL BOMBAS CAYERON EN LA CAPITAL. The headlines transparent. Except on the eternal bottom of the pyramid, expressions of outrage are everywhere, except on the bottom where hunger numbs even anger.

In Mexico's capital, which is teeming, which is sinking by inches, which is ringed by cardboard colonias, which are teeming, the day after the bombs have begun to drop on Baghdad, the florists are bringing their blooms to the heart, de costumbre, on Fridays, to the hotels and restaurants, the markets and sidewalk vendors.

And this Friday, no different, except the bombs are blooming in Baghdad, and in the heart of the capital of Old Mexico, which is sinking, the florists deliver to the zocalo, forming a quiet convoy, which stops traffic for miles, and the florists unload in early quiet, first light.

They empty their pungent cargo and begin to make a mosaic, which can be read by the guests in the Gran Hotel and the Majestic, which spells NO A LA GUERRA Y SI A LA PAZ. And the blooms left over which are given away to passersby.

And in Oaxaca City, on the roof of their hotel, looking over the zocalo: papier-mâché effigies, calla lilies, vigil by candle, graffiti on the walls of the gringo watering hole, and a wasted apparition circling the center, panhandling for smokes.

And in the following days the taxi drivers head for the Alameda, in Mexico City, flying pennants of peace from their aerials, and traffic, which is teeming, is stopped for miles. All quiet in the capital of the old Aztec Empire. Silence in the heart, habitat of 22,000,000 souls, which is sinking by centimeters. Which in inches equals eight a year.

Calla lilies limp in their buckets

The obligatory pariah dog

Concentrates its starved mass on a step

Blowflies battling the head

The casket seller checks

For occupancy before locking up

Monastery deep in shadow

Worker urinating into a box

Under the Bridge of Martyrs

Disposition of small limbs

A face dark and deadish

The petal of one eye shutting

In Hidalgo's courtyard

The pomegranate tree spreads

Into its memory of a future

For the next ones to forget

Ink of the padre's letters

Gone to vinegar

For the next ones to drink

Desk clerk mesmerized

By the new media-borne war

Hunting one legitimate spot to watch the world   crawl or limp along
                                        or cloud her air with no muffler

Whole new breed of dog born in every warren   the boy documenting them
            with his uninhibited lens

Wanting to be unsentimental about the mutt tethered to a leafless trunk without enough
                                        paid out to turn around

        The horse in the rubble of a wall lifting one encrusted hoof then the other

                Walks overflowing with merchandise

Man under worn awning hunched over old Singer mending pair of worn pants

                Kitten on the treadle being kitten

Shade and silence only near the chancel   as a hand can still all thoughts

                Basilica or no basilica   a beautiless town

The bus barreling down service roads to the hotels

Ashamed of her solace in being here   to be ashamed is to be American

                The boy leaving his merchandise in his seat

Two scorpions doing the merengue   the boy using his choplogic on her

Her hail of words directed against his tympana   fixes the attention of an anole
                                        on the ornamental iron

In their absence the house did not burn
the pipes were unfrozen

The dog did not suffer a drop of neglect

The glorious photographs of their son were not stolen
from their secondhand frames

Not so; instead

She is in the doorway wearing black on black
she is facing the fate she has always faced

She is shedding the strength in her arms
as the bones soften and thin

A faint diminishing signals an adumbration
as a feather passes under a nostril

Her ears are led to the tree she trusts, the cedar
still sensitive to its phantom limb

Reading on a ladder, she begins to tear
the pages from the sewn spine

Nary a death arrested nor a hair of a harm averted
by any scrawny farrago of letters

The air in the kitchen too small
air that would fit in a matchbox

The sun lukewarm and then a cold spot
in a colder-than-cold bed

As of Friday 850 of our members
will be   Forever Young

She burns bread and dislocates her TV
her all-American forgettery

Reading the obituaries, she counts
the ones older than her mother and father

Once in the alley avoids the fencing
between her and the albino dog

The true number of Iraqi dead to remain officially unknown
at the policy level no such estimates exist

The mind braying at the mind

A prescription for revulsion left in a taxi

A suffusion of color on a minimally disturbed surface
can calm the eye and the nerves

Our badly decomposed affairs are carted off
every other Wednesday

The writing in the trees remains illegible

Quietly, on Sunday,

in lieu of flowers

from poverty of divine direction

a crippling condition

watching a film a euphemism

for a bad movie watched before

a crippling condition

someone was coming to blow

away the fear

and names to be spoken

on her behalf

into a calabash

riding burro backwards

also cuts suffering

As if there were not other versions of the night
          the pressure increases

As if the strong were not empty and exhaustible
          the cavity inside her adjusts its light meter

As if the silence were not voluptuous in and of itself
          the outer wall repels the cold

As if the string light under his door meant he were waiting up
          how she had held her son   her suddenly-grown-tall son
             standing in the crosswalk in the drizzle

As if the scenery in her head had stopped revolving
          if she dodged the picture it is obvious his sweater was wet
                    his watch cap sopping

          As if the bone could not be pointed at the atrocious

As if they were ever going to quit catechizing everyone in sight
Her concerns fork out ahead of them   but given their fast-forward track
          and the national feelinglessness

As if all extravehicular activity were not now prohibited
What's going to become of us   is the beauty used up then

The momentum of lives shifts into the absence of thought
The first task is to recover the true words for being

In the event of our death   you will have to roll your own poetry

Inside an hour the thoughts of one would not be
        far from the thoughts of the other

As she searched for the origin of their bond
        her left arm felt somewhat numb

A coincidence had been coordinated by a friend
        of a friend at the Dark Dog

Or was it the fight over the negative balance

That fight was over in 126 seconds

Are we dying or did the power go out again

There passes my casket she says to no one

All of us are being conducted to a single point

One might say the same for plants

Do you have enough money for a taxi

Is my heavy hair still a comfort to you

I want you to burn every notebook, every disk,

Every ream, every scratch of my improvident pen

                    Until then,

Sick of their own vocabularies and the mud they bring in

Avoid the garrulous and unfortunately bald gringa   avoid
                                        all talk when possible

Lost among identical palms with a tropical drink   *sin hielo por favor*

German books in the lobby: *Alle glücklichen Familien ähneln einander; jede unglückliche*
                    aber ist auf ihre eigene Art unglücklich

The three of them under one moon forming a ligature: notes to be sung as one
                                        slur of words preserved in amber

Hair salt-stripped   only wind   burning to kiss her bent neck

Every regret its own cow to pick clean   as in: not tipping enough again

The boy out of film and pesos again   the woman waking up in full sun missing everyone

El Papa de Hitler propped upon an impressive chest   (Argentine?
                                        along the bias of her mind)

As soon as the boy swatted the fly then laid an ort of chocolate
                                        beside its stunned head

    it stutters and steers onto a nacreous walkway for takeoff

And a husbandly hand down her shirt expunging all references to disappointment

Minimally deluded it would stop   mercy out of nowhere like a wave banishing once more the old urge to speed off

by herself in a big red wreck

no matter where the local roads were going

In front of a donut shop   someone's son is shot dead

A witness on condition of anonymity

The slow open vulgar mouth   drawing on a cigarette

In a face once called Forever Young

Now to be known as Never-a-Man

Gone to the world of the working and the prevaricating

of the warring   world of drywalling of lousy test scores

of fishing from a bridge on a brilliant afternoon

          belt buckle blown undone

Recollect reading to her boy

reading to him in bed   overcome herself

with sleep as if drugged or slugged   then jabbed up again

Come on   Keep reading   Don't stop   Don't ever stop

like she was saying   Beauty cannot   she cannot marry

the Beast   and tonight as on all other rose-scented evens

He stumbles   the Beast he stumbles   from Beauty's empty chamber

In agony   he goes in agony   the fur of his fingers

smoking   until it's her boy he is the one saying

exclaiming   Yes Yes he will he will marry the Beast

          until he is the one who conks out

as a light pole struck by a drunken car

And suddenly it's raining like plastic

When she stumbles at last from the room

he is the one   who shakes himself awake

and yells   Protect me   and she is the one

who promises exclaiming   Yes Yes she will   I swear

if it kills me I will   as once the mother

of Forever Young shot in front of the donut shop

must have sworn   if it killed her she will   a boy

     So quiet   the reporter heard from his kin

You wouldn't even notice him on your electric bill

     Over there   it's a different world

     Desperate to be rejoined to this one

It is still raining like plastic

the brazen daytime rave of cicadae   cut off

In a fast fade to black   a low intensity shattering within

     to dramatize the break

Her confidential informant   is her imagination

Requests for him not to be photographed

in this position   not the flash of flesh

the powder burns that pepper the chest

You won't believe what I was dreaming

to the flash of flesh, the scarred back

                    (Do not think him healed)

Go back to sleep

It never happened

                    There was a cenote

and steps dug out of the centuries

                    and dogs always dogs

The hot iron on her chest she feels it now

It is her familiar   the fear   the sear

She is driving or is she   being driven

Trees and fences   fall behind   an oil truck

changes lanes   (without warning)

                    The water on her right looks dead

            bird sanctuary   void of birdsong

She forgets where she is headed   a meeting

No   an errand   an appointment   is her life

                comic or tragic   that card stays

facedown   she doesn't even know what hand

she's playing   or whose house belongs

                to the white rhododendron

Across the river   is a whole other world:

          Hotel (once grand) with a ballroom called Starlight

A lobby that smells like assisted-living dinner

          smoke-discolored chandelier

Aloe vera and bromeliad felted with dust

And toenails of the truly old painted
          for twirling across polished floors

And one of the old ones in a camphoric gown
          says she wore this when she was smaller

Spotlights on the fountain tinted for travelers
          in the time of terror   color of the koi

          Wasted figure in a tall mirror

          clad in ratty rags   forewarns

These are the last hours of empire or some such

inauspicious whispering   So?   What?   ¿So can I have a cigarette?

          (in the absence of any foreseeable remedy)

She ran off with a fallen aristocrat an adventurer
        cut down on his burro by bandidos

Belt blown undone   wrecked down there

When she came back to US
        they sent her son to Baghdad

whom she vowed to protect   if it kills her she will

There's not a troy ounce of compassion in this scenario

There is the inhuman dimension

The bridges breaking off in chunks
        of grey   libraries folding

School buildings indistinguishable from penitentiaries

Like I said to the doorman the other night

Some moon, huh

You should have seen it before the war Miss

We must not get used to this

to be cont.

The burros are not young   the macho a balker

The trail frays every which way

Coffee comes from bark

Tortillas made at dawn with a base of dust

Niguas bore into the soles

The brindle dog deserts

      Fleas

Cloth on the ceiling to catch scorpions

A mattress is unheard of

When there's no rawhide

A catre stretched with saplings

      Flies

A hot wind beats us off course

Warm beer or warm soda for supper

Ascent without end

Rumor of tigres and leones

These maps are worthless

      No supper

Fire moving this way

No corn for the burros

Cactus for privacy

       Ticks

Pigs are another bother

       No breakfast

The landmark mahogany struck down

The brindle returns

Running low on paregoric

       Snake

Cactus for shade

Running low on water

Smoking husks

The macho with an ulcerated back

One of us with dysentery y yo embarazada

A woman con pistola y cuchillo

Wears his trousers for comfort

Riding low

A boy the señora says

       Fifty pesos

Hands washed with mescal

He will pass out

In the corn crib

He will cut the cord he will

Cut it with his teeth

It devolved on her to speak through the shadows of events themselves:

       Animals or men passing through the night
al otro lado

       Without documents, blankets, contacts,
without water, without *with*

       Freeze, dehydrate, burn

       A knot of unmoving human forms
waiting for a bell to quicken them

       from pueblo without medicine maize or milk

       from colonia of cardboard without fuel or flour

Mira: you will never see faces like this again

These are the ones who loved you   these the ones who hurt

       Chihuahuan sun sizzles in its blackened trim

       Now moving at the speed of laudanum

Treading sand and dust under the big dry socket of god

Discarding the shawl   the straw hat that protected nada

       Desert floor entering memory hole

Ants beginning their business from the inside

       The drag road unavoidable

       Every footfall a giveaway unless

       One could vault out of the broken saddle
al otro lado   Farm Road 170

Without disturbing the particulate surface of earth
the way ghosts go back and forth

so that the famous black carriage of Juárez was also told to pass

Under the cover of tarbush
copperhead of their anonymity

Juan e Juana Doe
One last exhalation of earthly hell   breath chopped in half by a border

One last fata morgana   unless the reflection is not water but light

Unless the lights are the migra

Unless one does not know one could not in fact see to see

Unless one does not know that what one is hearing
is the simmer of one's very stomach in one's very blood   sopa de pollo

Dark meat breaking off in chunks

The last pinch of salt spent with the last wick of sweat

Unless one does not know that what one is hearing
is the crashing of one's skeleton   chandelierlike

Like they say in Iraq   Now fear up harsh

I was just thinking

I hadn't worn a dress in so long   the current between my legs

witching as I head for the truck   library shutting ahead of time

clock set to remember something   cars abandoned on the off-ramp

plows forming a convoy on Wampanoag Trail   in advance of the whiteout

juncos blown through frantic branches   snow disappearing the rhododendron

Allied military reports

Deadliest day for the forces   Super Stallion crash   not

counting the number of their dead   no such estimates exist

sandstorms on the AccuWeather map   near Ar Rutba

in the western region   town of 22,000   not counting their dead

In his suddenly-grown-small room   the boy freestyling to lifted beats

Telling him through the door   The dog has to go out now

turn down the freaking sound   and No Fumar in the house

The handle turning clockwise   the hood obscures all

but the slow open mouth   These are not the limits of my world but the limits of my words tonight   He is writing something down

he does not care to share   folding the paper over with cold hands

to be cont.

Like the Sun Down There

Early in the day they were driving past the small vineyard.

They were looking forward to walking around in another town.

They could find a wrought-iron bench in a garden of splashy flowers.

They might find a swimming hole.

Just beyond the vineyard they passed a dog standing against the body of a dog.

They passed a number of one-story houses sprouting rebar from the rooftops.

A man balancing bundles on his handlebars.

Plastic bags caught in organ cactus.

The town was twisted and steep.

The streets cobbled and shops full of punched tin.

They sat on a wall and watched children play in the dust.

At the waterworks women were washing mounds of colored clothing.

A man walking his hog by a length of hemp knocked on a door in an exterior wall and was let in.

They walked down some steps into a candlelit room.

The closeness, the warmth, the voices of people eating together.

The sound of plates slowly being stacked and a bird in the kitchen.

The disconsolate strain of a traditional song.

The full and weary ride home.

Just before the vineyard

the lights of the car picked out the standing dog, the body of the other one.

Like a Prisoner of Soft Words (1)

We walk under the wires and the birds resettle.

We know where we're going but have not made up our mind

which way we will take to get there.

If we pass by the palmist's she can read our wayward lines.

We may drop things along the way that substantiate our having been here.

We will not be able to transmit any of these feelings verbatim.

By the time we reach the restaurant one of us is angry.

Here a door gives in to a courtyard

overlooking a ruined pool.

We touch the spot on our shirt where the ink has seeped.

The lonely outline of the host is discerned near an unlit sconce.

Something about an oar leaning against a wall.

As guests we are authorized not to notice.

We lack verisimilitude but we press on with intense resolve.

We arc forced to admit we cannot reproduce the smell of the linden.

But we can tell you when we are standing

in the sphere of its fluency, its mystery, its heart-shaped leaves,

its special white honey, the precarious fabric of its protection.

We appear less posthumous

against the silver exposures. When the wind picks up

the sound track isn't audible.

Rising, Falling, Hovering,

cont.

Rising, Falling, Hovering,

cont.

Floods of feelings

militarize our nights   currents of solitude   cordon off

our days   Oct 16   the famous Carousel Bar reopened

in the Crescent City   customers resumed drinking

revolving and sinking   Providence continues to launch

hurtle heave its leaves   And as of Sat Nov 12

according to the Associated Press   2,066

of our members   will remain Forever Young

O when the saints go
marching

At the level   of policy   their kids   don't exist

never did   will never reach   the sun-drenched shore

and now it's Monday again

I have been to Pilates   I found my old coat

I took my will to the notary   I found my good glasses

I have filled my tank   I am going to the market

then I think I'll cut my hair off with a broken bottle

                                        As of three hours ago

2,311 of our members are to remain   Forever Young

We'll be in Mexico City in under five   we're going back

Our friend has started her treatment   so we are going

We still have pesos   there's a Pullman from the airport

          Who was down last you or me

Now you have to go upstairs   No   you go down

He tells her to turn off the light   though he has his own light

And it is switched off   Hers is cocked oddly

It illumines the gutter of the book   at the margins it fails

He tunes into his iPod   the black mask covers his eyes

He has furled his body toward the window of the craft

The shade is down all the way   she prefers to see out

If she could extend an arm through the porthole and pull the clouds over them

                                        O Heavenly Comforter

Let's get that light off   You aren't really reading   The monitor from the overhead

begins its infotainment   Not shown: white phosphorus   falling

on the city of minarets

Not confirmed: the use of white phosphorus   (for another year) NOW SHOWING:

CAT WOMAN   If you cannot or do not wish to perform the function

You must change seats now

Was it only last summer they sent their son   their suddenly-grown-tall son

to Cuauhnahuac   to finish the summer   (otherwise would the summer's son

withstand the son's mother   or: the blood-stopping words they swapped)

to study Spanish   This was when the job helping the carpenter

who didn't need much help   dwindled to holding the ladder

Picked up at the bus station by their friend

who has finished her second treatment whose hair

doesn't fall out until the day after their departure

but this was before the bad diagnosis

The boy wouldn't hear of staying with their friend of course

It was too close to family too close to knowing his business

He wanted to stay in the rojo district   To save money he said

He stayed in a private house renting out rooms   partway up the hill   in the Pradera

directly across the barranca   from the donkey that never stopped hawing

His wife di-et   the proprietor talked through a mechanical larynx

meaning the jenny was dead and the macho was all broken up

Threw his duffel onto his bed   stashed his checks in a drawer   took a taxi

to the language school (routinely taking taxis)   registered   met someone
                                                    (name of Al)

hopped on a second-class bus   and rode through the howling Mexican night

swerving around heifers on the sun-warmed asphalt

        the night permanently deep   the stars permanently powered

Changing buses in the pueblo where years ago   (before the son existed

as a thought in the body)   his parents stopped   they caught a band of young

shirtless men breaking into their car   siesta time   and the men in full sun

backed away from the vehicle   hands up in front of them   backing away

when they realized as the couple walked slowly downhill

in their direction they were the ones   who belonged to the car with Arkansas plates

                        Until he reached the Pacific

Her fear   as always   was that he would make it

to the bottommost level of the underworld   where the smoke has no way out

So the scared self assembles around the stiff self

And the son's mother withstands the summer's son (and vice versa)

      (If you cannot or do not wish to perform
      this function   you shouldn't be in this century)

Anyway he and call-him-Al   someone he had met fifteen minutes before

they went to the station and bought tickets   rode the bus

to Zihuatanejo   before the night was over his wallet was lost

something he only discovered when they pulled over

in that pueblo where his parents almost had an incident   and so was his friend's

dependent at least until he could get back to Cuauhnahuac a few hours before class

They don't learn if the boys even had time for a swim

in the shallow sharky water   or some fried steak and cebollas

at an open-air stand   before they had to catch the return bus

A town where they themselves had ordered flattened steaks and onions

and stood in the rain in an open-air theater and watched a cast-of-eyes movie with Bedouins and who-knows-who-else   The celluloid crackling

The rain warm but hard falling

But the son and call-him-Al actually did get back and make it to class on Monday

Está comiendo mi coco she phoned the friend

who had picked him up at the station

who had never heard the expression she was so pleased with herself for using

from a dated phrase book   This phrase is never used in Mexico her friend assured

He is still eating my head

If you give your fears a shape   her friend suggested

you break free of them   This was before the bad diagnosis

After she is assured he is back   from the sea

she concedes   He is going to be OK   He'll make his way

Recalls a woman she met at the women's prison   the literacy teacher

(not an inmate) who had several ex-husbands under her belt

and had one son (not by the federal judge) (that husband didn't hunt)

but by the one who sold indigenous rugs   the son from that marriage

A very fastidious boy   always in the shower always changing

from one white shirt into another   she worried about him

she came in the house one day and smelled squirrel

He swerved he said but still hit it   he thought it would be a pity

to leave in the road   so he brought it home   skinned and rubbed

its still soft body down with oil and rosemary   stuck it in the broiler

He'll be OK   she thought   this fastidious son   He'll make his way

During the time she knew he was on a bus   without a wallet   she knew this much

because he left a message on her machine   hurtling as Mexican buses tend to go

she could only say   Está comiendo mi coco   He is eating my head

                                                 He was gone

        Her breath clouds the pane   of a second-story window

        she watches the silver Matrix with a bent fender   key scratch

        along a diagonal   the driver's side   backing out of its cove

        Birds folding up   a glimpse of the coyote that's been patrolling

        the perimeter as it cuts into the burial ground   She sits in the cold

        staring at a cigarette coming apart in a glass of water

At this writing he's finishing a year in college

Also at this writing the smoking thing has been supplanted

by the gym thing   he has joined an underground fight club

and she worries about him nonstop   You see yourself

wearing a championship belt   Mister BLING

holding up a fist of greenbacks   I see myself

being taught how to insert the feeding tube

Don't you see how our visions do not correspond

(Todavía está comiendo mi coco)

He mentions getting jumped in Zihuatanejo and cornered the year before in Oaxaca

the Christmas before in Chicago and mugged once in Brooklyn

and she is What What What   Can't you just stay inside and read
(turning pages)

until you're thirty or something

In Mexico she smoked

Smoke Smoke her friend says

If this is the fifth sun we're all going up

The Pullman descends
The helix of Cuauhnahuac
Hurtling toward the station
Oh look Media Naranja
A new Walmex

His face unfurls furls
Poetry
Doesn't
Protect
You
Anymore

The house dormant   She feels her way to the toilet among the shadows

wall of masks   in shadow   wall of books

open hearth   piano crouched under stairs   in shadow

Before the city is clogged with exhaust and the ravines

streaming with orangey water and sewage   before the dogs start barking

She steps out into a fast-lifting cloud   an earliness of light filtering

through the eucalyptus leaves   she sees what she knew to be there but seldom

could be seen

and she stumbles back through the dark forest of furniture to tell him

What is He doing.

Smoking.

And Izta, what is She doing.

Sleeping.

As (so) was I.

¿Mande?

Nada.

And when she rushes back to the stone porch, the volcano is gone.

A minor fiesta blocks off one road

Another way is found

From their table on the mezzanine

A view of the mosaic

Diego did or did not draw

Of Gaia in the floor of the pool

In the once weekend house

Of the beloved Cantinflas

Gaia swirling underwater

A curtain of bougainvillea

Tumbling down the corner wall

Of the open courtyard

Their beautiful unruly friend

Unusually subdued

Her rebozo swaddling

Her thin limbs

Her intravenous access

Her husband has returned

From a fertility conference

This very evening

The faint whine of mosquitoes

Brings a joven to light the citronella

In Kyoto   he is telling them

In a department store

A persistent sound

Became intolerable to him

He asked a clerk

Could she make it stop

(It was eating his head)

A pitch said the astonished woman

Only dogs are supposed to hear

A chain of tiny explosions

In the direction of the fiesta

Reveals a moon under construction

According to the Gaia hypothesis, the earth is alive;

According to Lieutenant Colonel Venable white phosphorus
          is not a chemical weapon, it's an incendiary.

It is an obscurant, it is for illumination;
          nor are we a signatory of any treaty restricting its use.

Not so many scientists subscribe to the Gaia hypothesis.

Nor are so many rushing to refute the thousand and one levels of interdependence.

Elsewhere a suicide car bomber struck a police station.
Killing at least one and wounding seven.
Gunmen also killed a teacher near his home.
The bakeries become targets. The saints removed from the walls.
For protection. One who was kidnapped and tortured.
And dumped with thirteen dead bodies.
And a barber shop was ambushed killing two including the owner.
A tire repairman was shot dead.
And one who refused to change the ring on his cell phone.
They put four bullets in his head.
Spoken anonymously. For fear of reprisals.
And an analyst. For the Center.
You get enclaves and fortresses.
People become violent to the people outside.

If a body makes 1 centavo per chile picked or
5 cents for 50 chiles can Walmex get it down to 3 cents. Pass the savings on to US.
Will they open a Supercenter in Fallujah once it is pacified. Once the corpses
in the garden have decomposed. Once the wild dogs have finished off the bones.
Does the war never end. Is this the war of all against all.
Who will build the great wall between us, the illegals, the vigilantes, the evangelicals

or the ones who come back from Fallujah with four limbs and attached head.
And the Supercenter in Teotihuacán. Is it not quietly being built at the skirt
of the pyramids. Will the great job of the future be The Greeter.
Thus did Montezuma open his arms to Cortés.
In a gesture Prescott referred to as Montezuma's nonresistance to evil.
Thus did one terrible story begin to unfold. De costumbre.

(This would have been during

Operation hold the line Operation don't drink

French wine Operation embed the press and

let them wear the sexy new gear   Operation burn the boots

with the sand niggers' feet inside   Operation product endorsement

Operation permanent party   Operation it depends

upon how you define the word torture [acts must be of an extreme nature
                                                    to rise to the level

of torture… organ failure impairment of bodily function, even death]

Operation phantom fury Operation white phosphorus

[in our hands] is not a chemical weapon

but an incendiary an obscurant an illumination and an important
                                                    psychological weapon

Operation wedding party massacre

Operation liar liar pants on fire and [the culturally sensitive]

Operation enduring freedom)

64

The next day they are heading al otro lado

A centipede is killed with a book

The santo of Peregrine has been moved

El Popo is smoking

Behind a brown scrim of exhaust

When everyone drops their reserve

Everyone is thinking about the end of things

The next day the treatments resume

Her skin she would tell her later on the phone

Feels as if it had been in a kiln

Our lot bounded

By a busy road at the foot

Of the hill

Here and here

By burial ground #34

When a veteran—

Bagpipes and guns—

The dog throws up

On the Oaxacan rug

If at the window I watch

The flag being folded and

Gently tendered

To the woman in the front

Lately they were younger

These women

Children standing about

In dark clothes

It could happen like this

To someone you know

I am not saying it will

I am saying it could

Just as I overheard

Someone ask

Less than a month ago

How is your son

A woman mumble

He is in a better place

In which case   there's nothing

More to say   is there

Is rage your issue

Well is it   Is it

As the earth heats up

People are moving north

Fragmentary partial contradictory

Unconstrained by facts

Phrases cycling through us as routine as prison meals:

Politics are an aspect
Business is good
We are rushing about to meet the demands of our lives
How do you want your chicken

Philosophy isn't transcendent
Who told you that
The imagination has been tamed
Friendship is irrelevant
Fragile is life
Everyone is alone here
History disappears
Quality cannot be controlled
All bets are off

As of Wednesday morning 2,845 of our members completed the Circle of Life
Epidemiologists from here and there estimate 600,000 civilian dead
About 15,000 a month, a number swiftly dismissed by the White House

Just once I'd like to watch a movie up here that contains violence graphic language torture
simulated sex cruelty to animals rape library-burning white-phosphorus shelling illegal military
recruiting wanton profiteering artifact-looting and more

What I want is a closed-captioned-surround-sound-UV-protected Armageddon

Rage could be my issue

                              And so I have come to want them—
them being, those people, the current occupants of 1600 Pennsylvania,
I can't even bear to say their [expletive] monosyllabic surnames
for dread of it calling up their bland [expletive] faces; yet I have come
to want them, almost obsessively come to want them, to exist in this dread:
for the nondescript car to pull up and disgorge the uniformed men

with their generic words tapped out of their well-drilled heads;
for the blunted bodies of this couple to be riveted to this dread,
for their blunted minds to stick on this expectation as if driven into
their bones of the natural order upended—that their twins are dead. No,
that their twins are blessed to give of themselves so selflessly in this struggle
for our way of life as it is so correctly, so vulgarly called; though I do not want
them to actually receive this news to actually have the twins be dead,
nor for their eyes to be blacked out, nor their earthly functions
be stopped, nor their blood to quit flowing to their temporal lobes,
but I sincerely do want this couple this very couple, the current occupants,
to exist solely, wholly in this dread. Because we do.

Before the landscape asserts its unexaggerated loveliness

box buildings and a pipe fitters union hall

its diode streaming patriotic messages

the billboard announcing an unclaimed jackpot

oil trucks barreling toward the company security gate

he is the one driving

she is absently counting storage tanks on her right

and noting the cars pulled over at the homosexual trysting point

the bird sanctuary   void of birdsong

before Hundred Acre Cove swerves into sight

the stark silhouette of the osprey nest on its platform

his hand relaxing over the wheel   saying he is glad they went   glad

to be back   that he loved living

in the old school   not in but near the city

with the wormy fruit trees   the burial ground next door

and that he thinks about our son constantly

Later (de costumbre)
a moon would appear

Like Having a Light at Your Back You Can't See but You Can Still Feel (2)

As if it were streaming into your ear.

The edges of a room long vanished.

She is not really hearing what he's really saying.

The shine is going out of the ground
but they are sure of their footing.

They have been here a thousand and one times.

There are masses of rose hips and they are noisy.

The forward direction requires almost no effort.

Consonant with this feeling of harmony
comes another, less comfortable.

Not of being lost but of not belonging.

Yet they were not covering the space
with false words.

They moved along without talking,
not touching.

They wore their own smell. The air
was salty.

Others were out there who were drifting.

It is a bay in New England
closed to shellfishing after heavy rains.

The house is not far from here. Next to the old
burial ground.

Most nights aren't dark enough to see stars.

If a bad movie, a bad movie. If a bad meal,
a bad meal. If bad wine, bad wine.

They read. And go to bed early. He puts on an eyemask.

She wants a light on. She wants to read.

No, he says. Turn it off.

Let me finish the chapter.

Turn it off, C.

The page then, she says. You have your mask on.

I can still feel it, he says. I can feel it

streaming in my ear. Besides,

he is adamant,

you just go to sleep at night

I go on a journey.

Like the Hour of Our Perfection

Whereas before things were all immanence,
now were they all valence

in the breathing world where we met.

Who presented initial shyness.

Who disheveled the light at the threshold.

With a look of near-adolescence, so one did not know
if he also slept with the men.

And the ledge of a hip when

seen first from behind, a voice, an outline.

And the breast spared after an early scare.

Her amulet of dead rosesuckers.

Her black hollyhocks soaring to the second story.

His lemons cut into eight precise slices.

A door hung by which one could leave if one chose to go.

Always movement, hypotheticals, another qualm.

The dashes of footprints after a shower.

I'm not saying it did happen.

I'm saying it could have it could have happened like this.

Like something of ivory so scarce
and procured with such violence.

What fell as a fine rug receives a harp.

Like Things That Might Go On in Infinite Dimensions

Let the tail of the dog lead: a suspicious man is walking west

dressed all in white. Cardinal numbers shall defer to ordinal. A suspicious letter

arrives in an unknown hand. A glass of water is drunk, a candle sputters; something

goes pop. Every unexpected sound shall be investigated.

THE MEDIUM IS FEAR

Cholera persists, even here. Sincerely, Ursa Minor, have you seen my ankh.

A man dressed all in black is walking northbound, his eyes set close together. A fight

breaks out in aisle 13 of Wal-Mart and someone is masturbating in the reptile section.

The scent on her comb disappears.

LOSS IS THE MESSAGE

An anonymous caller reports: loud music and goat sacrifices on Old Wire Road.

The dog blows its hair. Between scattered showers and a power outage, this and this

happened. A man reports his surveillance camera stolen and a new motherboard installed.

Now, get out of that silly Ghillie suit, before you are taken for a foreigner.

THE MEDIUM IS CLEAR

In heaven, beds are turned down between six and seven; Thursday marks

the deaths of a retired grocer, a homemaker, a retired plumber, and a quality-control

worker. Salvation being local, our gradual dissolution huffs into view.

Constant effort is required, a pound of thrust for every pound

of anything else just to hold our own against the forces. Promise me one thing. Promise

you won't go home with Nosferatu, the mothers tell their sixteen-year-olds

amid a flurry of warnings

Like a Prisoner of Soft Words (2)

We walk under the wires and the birds resettle.

We know where we're going but have not made up our mind

which way we will take to get there.

If we pass by the palmist's she can read our wayward lines.

We may drop things along the way that substantiate our having been here.

We will not be able to transmit any of these feelings verbatim.

By the time we reach the restaurant one of us is angry.

Here a door gives in to a courtyard

overlooking a ruined pool.

We suspect someone has followed one or the other of us.

We touch the spot on our shirt where the ink has seeped.

The lonely outline of the host is discerned near an unlit sconce.

As guests we are authorized not to notice.

We drop some cash on the tablecloth.

We lack verisimilitude but we press on with intense resolve.

At the border, under a rim of rock, the footbridge.

Salt cedars have grown over the path.

The water table is down.

And we cannot see who is coming, the pollos and their pollero,

the migra, the mules, the Minutemen, the women

who wash for the other women al otro lado.

Or the murdered boy herding his goats after school. 6:27,

the fell of dark, not day.

Or: Animism

We have degenerated into people—DUO DUO

We are back from the ark, almost.

Is it always this dark?

Who was here first?

Since it is so lush why does everything have that chemistry-set smell?

Is there still time for a crisis?

It rained. Or did it? There is water yet standing.

When in the late afternoon, everything gets hungry.

If my head should fall off, please don't put it in a sack.

Does one start with the face. Save the jam for the end?

The sign said GRAVEDIGGING TWO BODIES A DAY

SIXTY CENTS AN HOUR.

How does one decide what to leave for the others?

If the cheese were all that is left

how would that be ascribable to me?

When the light doesn't cover itself up

then will you see the incision of my words?

We are back from the dark, almost.

What is a savanna anyway?

Dogs everywhere are close kin. Like Amish.

Jesus, the Cistercian biology teacher told them, had 23 chromosomes

and was the spit and image of his mother.

Carcass of love, carrion of the wedding feast.

Go ahead, pick my bones.

I dreamed I was biting his arm.

I dreamed he was taking me to Nebraska on foot

for our honeymoon. And this was the best I'd felt in a long time.

Those who question the primacy of the phallus

are surely in for it.

It stopped raining. But made no discernible difference.

The thirst was and will be with us forever.

And after the dogs, the others would come.

First two, then more; in pairs, then more.

And the hewed stones form a pair as well. Blackened. Fallen.

Perhaps from a monument. A marker for a significant boundary.

Toppled. Here in the savanna.

Because it is beautiful you should not walk alone.

Because it is beautiful you should not go without shoes.

But take a long look. For the rest of nature is nearly morte.

When I think of dying. I think of the ultimate release from fear.

When I think of dying, I get so scared my body refuses to lie down.

There is always time for a crisis.

      Even here, another Fourth, everyone is prey to the heat
and the drums. Cars supplant the beasts.

      Where was he. He said he would be back before the clouds
broke. And the headlights began streaming down County Road.

      Or he would stay until the final minutes before the finale and
the cars became belligerent and began to degenerate into people.

      He knew the ark would not wait.

      He knew they were booked to the rafters.

      He knew we could lose our cheap seats in the reaches
where the Juilliard students stand up reading the scores.

And therefore, we have to wait for the hyenas to get hungry

enough to kill for their supper. Then we will come

with our napkins tucked under our chins

and our cutlery gleaming. Things seem more eternal

elsewhere. Where one eats until one is eaten.

　　　　Never eat to be eating.

　　　　There was a sheen on the road soon after we entered

the city limits. The air, splendid, freshly wetted.

　　　　Have you ever attempted to count the storage tanks when you

passed them on the way back. Have you ever reeled

under the magnitude of petroleum's ruin.

The beast involuntarily turns its rack of ribs up for the pack.

He has pulled into the breakdown lane, burning oil.

If these rags are edible, we will live.

I am the last one in the house to go to bed.

Listen. The insects resume where the fireworks left off.

Or, if not, the insects collect at the light

with their silent scores.

Isn't the engine turning over. Almost.

There must be a reset button for this machine.

Let's be realistic. We are never coming back.

Like the Ghost of a Carrier Pigeon

In a couple of hours darkness will throw its blanket

over the scene   she will pretend to read a mystery
                    the mower and hammering will cease

The bees leave the andromeda and then

So much has been spent constructing a plausible life
she did not hear the engines of dissent run down

Some still attempt to cover the skull with the wire of their hair
                    others shave everything instead

A solitary relives the pleasure of releasing his bird

There is no sacrosanct version   there is only time

Even now   if someone yells Avalanche   she has one
Thoughts shudder against the ribs and go still

Soon the son would be out running around in her car
with a sore throat   soon the decibels commence killing off hair cells

She checks to see if the phone is charged and then

The ones responsible for slaying the dreamer are mostly in the ground
but the ones responsible for slaying the dream

suffer only metabolic syndrome

Even now   now that her supply of contact lenses has dwindled
                            she was refusing to sing the Wal-Mart song

The bees would be back and then

All efforts at reconciliation aside   even if everyone exchanged germs
                            happiness is only for amateurs

A dress worn only once before has been hung on the door
                            the mirror under the cloth receives its image

Like Something Christenberry Pictured

If this were not a marked beginning, but an end or more severely, *the end,* and you were ready to make peace with your major failures and hidden contradictions, and you were about to start the countdown on your own long-lived-in body (and so,

a little flyover in remembrance),

you would seem alert enough to attend this imminent loss, sensing your own twirl in the void accelerating toward its outermost ring while your sputtering mind starts its rewind of the crud-and-gem-encrusted strata through which poetry has taken you as if some kook might jump out of the holly at any moment and extinguish you with one stroke;

hit pause before contact is made between your phantom assailant and your individual quote unquote soul and you are physically hied to a ramshackle building risen in full sun from uncut grass, the walls stripped of canned and dried goods and a single stick insect sticking to a tatter of color on a post struggling to support a torn roof

(like something Christenberry pictured);

fast-forward to glimpse last-year's-tired-of-sitting self in a coarse concrete hall, anemic palette and dais of drowsy party officials; a withered wand of a woman facing the audience, the foreigners, holding her granddaughter's hand reciting the *Manas* by the hundreds of lines, and the expressionless girl picking up when her infallible hand is squeezed, thus transmitting to her infallible memory the epic of her people;

mesmerizing until it's unbearable when you hit forward again to edge your rental car off the shoulder so you can photograph with your cell phone an alligator snapper crossing the road so poky the sixteen-wheeler that barrels over it blows the moss from its back and it freezes in position to recover from the sudden ventilation, then picks up tempo just enough to clear the truck bearing down in the opposite direction;

it tips over the edge of blacktop

under the unfinished garage of sky toward a section of river where nothing much is moving in a stand of cypress making a final stand against the final clearing of an exhausted land and you half expect to be chosen, to be the one to glimpse the trailing feathers of the bird no one has been able to vouch for, which is why you chose the tertiary route through empty corduroy fields the instant you stopped

at the crossroads, as they say, which was the very instant you stopped looking for meaning and began rifling among the folds of feeling instead where things were to be made new again, where and when the benighted and unresponsive have begun to lose their grip even on and unto the benighted and unresponsive

It is like waking up

to the old-fashioned smell of roses

it's like finding a few words

collected on the eyes

of visiting moths; like giving of your blood, generously

to live and die

as if the same occasion

having never owned a catamaran

but having cooled off in Bright Angel Creek

danced slo-mo at the Night Spot

sped through the hot air

past the second-story wedding dress stores

of San Luis Potosí

having stayed up to watch the cereus open

the last time it bloomed twelve years ago

when the boy was still a boy when

the elevator doors opened on

a once-elegant man

playing *Rhapsody in Blue*

on the mezzanine of a once-elegant hotel

having cruised alongside

the Big Woods at 12mph

straining to glimpse

an apparition of a wing

Ah, the flesh flashes and passes

so simple and satisfying as drinking milk

out of the carton or going from

maddeningly boring stretches (in front of a monitor)

to eating clouds (faintly lit within)

burning pages of bad poetry

stepping out of the story

(ineluctably over, fellow travelers)

here just long enough to testify

to a blinding intensity

under that big dry socket of god

the camera mounted to capture

ordinary traffic violations

fixes instead on your final face

a single frame of unadulterated

urgency is what you see, urgency it is

Like Something Flying Backwards

When a word here and there was starting to escape.

There is some hope that she may yet.

Even by herself could work herself into a fit.

Often thought of death in daylight before washing, before touching a switch.

Written purely out of love for the calm it offered—for to calm someone else is calming, whether or not one can calm oneself.

If never delivered never so intended.

Her vocabulary refined by years of looking through the screen at the lilac that absorbed her witness.

So many contradictory measures taking up their positions.

The ubiquitous sense of scarcity especially where there was plenty.

So much turbulence in choosing.

She had to jimmy her way in.

Even an attempt to change her seating assignment.

All of her experience still looking for a language.

Honestly if she were able she would haul in one of the more animate clouds.

The following spring she promised herself to plant a white lilac.

She would take up her old position, hands folded, head back
waiting for the visions.

End Thoughts

In the beginning the usual dark dark of very dark
In a few years there appears a crack in the dark a very small crack
The crack as I said appears very small
          and jagged as cracks are

The temperature has already been adjusted
          by the state
Our obsolescence built into the system

When you use the ladies' room
          do not put your purse on the floor
When the civilian words are dispensed
          different meanings will be assigned
The new meanings will be fired
          at the head and groin area

For instance saying Can't a girl get anything to eat around here
would now signify Water with a stomach wound is fatal
Or if you were to say The mariachis are coming
          it would be interpreted as Just open the f__g trunk

All extroverted activity will be suspended
          in residential zones
Absolutely no tea parties under the trees

Crying helps
Crying doesn't help

One wants to make oneself smaller than the mouse
under the icebox One wants to dry into invisible ink

One has a sense of something out there that needs saving
            and one ought to attach the buckle
to a heavy-gauge wire and pull him through

Waking up knowing this much is not the hard part
nor lifting the head from its existential drift
            it's the sticking of one's foot off the edge
            lowering it to the cold floor

and finding the correct instrument
to work that crack into a big enough opening
            to venture forward

Before the fall no story after the fall the old story
After the fires floods along with serpents and bugs
After the floods years of drought
After drought just dusk which is when everything
            really begins to hurt

            and then there is the human dimension

Like Something in His Handwriting

It was hotter back then.

No, it wasn't it had to be cooler, clouded.

A park down below where no one ever met.

But men were pulled by dogs along paths made by the walkers.

And a nameless river through a photograph of woods

proposed a nonlocal reality

that shimmered at the instant of its own disappearance.

She bought the picture, brought it back, propped it against drywall

where someone had penciled a message

she couldn't make out.

The end of another summer wandered across yards

that weren't fenced or watered.

If it rained, it rained.

And then the rain inebriated us.

A yellow leaf floated toward ground

transmitting a spot of optimism

through a slow intensification of color in the lower corner of the morning.

Notes

Our world the world of colors is *the* world.—JULIAN BECK

"Can you describe this. / I cannot." References (in the negative) Anna Akhmatova's "Instead of a Preface," from *Requiem.*

On pages 22 and 30 are reworkings of a text composed for a collaboration, titled *Ligature,* with poet Forrest Gander and sculptor Douglas Culhane.

"the national feelinglessness" is an expression of Julian Beck's. It appears in *daily light daily speech daily life* (1984), translated by Riccardo Duranti into Italian for bilingual publication.

"That fight was over in 126 seconds" alludes to the famous match between Sonny Liston and Floyd Patterson, September 25, 1962, Chicago.

"Alle glüklichen Familien ähneln einander; jede unglückliche aber ist auf ihre eigene Art unglücklich" is a German translation of the first line of *Anna Karenina,* which I jotted down when leafing through a bookshelf in the open-air lobby of a hotel in the Dominican Republic. Translated by Fred Ottow.

"Pigs are another bother" appears in *Where the Strange Roads Go Down* (1953), Mary del Villar and Fred del Villar's account of their journey on foot through the Tierra Caliente of Mexico in 1951. "These maps are worthless" appears in the text in Spanish as "no servía para nada."

The revered Zapotec president, Benito Juárez, from the Valle de Oaxaca, battled for justice his entire adult life. During the French invasion of Mexico, he had to keep moving to avoid assassination; so the seat of his government was a black carriage.

"one could not in fact see to see" is adapted from the last line of Emily Dickinson's "I heard a Fly buzz—when I died."

Sopa de pollo ("chicken soup") is used because one term for undocumented emigrants from Mexico is pollo; their smuggler, pollero. A gruesome description of the human body's stage-by-stage collapse in failed crossings is found in *Devil's Highway* (2004), by Luis Alberto Urrea.

One puts oneself to the pain of reading the papers. Phrases on page 42 were borrowed from one article by Sabrina Tavernise, Friday, July 21, 2006, *New York Times*.

"These are not the limits of my world / but the limits of my words tonight" of course rephrases Wittgenstein's famous dictum, "The limits of my language mean the limits of my world," variously translated as "The limits of my language are the limits of my mind," 5.6 of *Tractatus Logico-Philosophicus*.

Cuauhnahuac ("near the forest") is the Nahuatl name for the city the Spanish renamed Cuernavaca ("cow's horn").

"Poetry / Doesn't / Protect / You / Anymore" references (by substitution) a phrase in a diode from *The Survival Series*, by Jenny Holzer, installed at the Mildred Lane Kemper Art Museum at Washington University in St. Louis.

The volcanoes overlooking Cuauhnahuac and rimming the Valle de México are Iztaccíthuatl ("white woman," also translated as "sleeping woman") and Popocatépetl ("smoking mountain").

Cantinflas, Mario Moreno Reyes, a big-eared, nonsense/speed talking film comedian, was heralded as the world's greatest by no less than Chaplin. He made over fifty films in Spanish, and in English played the valet Passepartout in *Around the World in 80 Days* (1956).

William H. Prescott's page-turner, *History of the Conquest of Mexico*, was published in 1843.

ADDITIONALLY:

On p. 78, Hopkins gets the last line.

"Like Something Christenberry Pictured" was written for Harvard's two hundred and seventeenth Phi Beta Kappa Literary Exercises, June 5, 2007. It was published in *Conjunctions: #49, A Writers' Aviary*.

Notes on the notes: I might have included other notes, but I lost my notebook in the Barrington Public Library, February 19, 2005. (And that was that time.) While my preference is to include notes in a more interesting compositional form than I have done here, no such design offered itself up.

About the Author

C.D. Wright has published over a dozen works of poetry and prose. Among her honors are the Robert Creeley Award and a MacArthur Fellowship. She lives outside of Providence.

The Chinese character for poetry is made up of two parts: "word" and "temple." It also serves as pressmark for Copper Canyon Press.

Since 1972, Copper Canyon Press has fostered the work of emerging, established, and world-renowned poets for an expanding audience. The Press thrives with the generous patronage of readers, writers, booksellers, librarians, teachers, students, and funders—everyone who shares the belief that poetry is vital to language and living.

Major funding has been provided by:

Anonymous (2)

Sarah and Tim Cavanaugh

Beroz Ferrell & The Point, LLC

Lannan Foundation

LEF Foundation

National Endowment for the Arts

Cynthia Lovelace Sears and Frank Buxton

Washington State Arts Commission

For information and catalogs:

COPPER CANYON PRESS
Post Office Box 271
Port Townsend, Washington 98368
360-385-4925

Set in Adobe Caslon, a font designed by Carol Twombly based on the English Baroque typefaces of William Caslon. Display type set in Bell. Book design by Valerie Brewster, Scribe Typography. Printed on archival-quality paper at McNaughton & Gunn, Inc.